Gc
Building Confidence Daily

Dr. Shelly-Ann Gajadhar
L.L.B., L.E.C.,
MSc., Pg.Dip., PhD

———————

Eternal Sunshine, LLC
P.O. Box 888225
Dunwoody, GA 30356

INTRODUCTION

I remember on my first day of law school being shocked that I qualified. I always dreamed to be an attorney but now, I was actually in the moment. There were a flood of emotions I felt from anxiety to excitement and it was difficult to put into words. Once I got dressed for the day I reached for a daily inspirational book that my mom gave me at 17. I flipped to the relevant date, sat on the bed and allowed the inspirational quote of the day to sink in. They were words that I needed. Words that my soul hoped to hear and though my family and friends tried their best, the words of the book always showed up for me. Maybe because I was in a different place from most. I was a first generation university student, first in my family to study abroad, first in my family to do my PhD and first of many other things. I dreamt big and my attitude can be described as "going bravely in everything I desired in this life". That daily inspirational book that my mother gave me at age 17 still gets referenced by me ever so often in my mid-30's and though dated and worn it was the inspiration for this book.

Dreaming big, outgrowing spaces and listening to your soul's calling is tough work for a society that constantly says "no" and "you cannot". I wrote this book so that all dreamers feel seen, supported and celebrated on the daily. Between the pages of this book, you will find more confidence in pursuing your dreams and honoring your soul's desires. I hope that you feel less alone, less misunderstood and more empowered to confidently pursue your dreams. You were designed for something great and this book this book is here to remind you of that on the daily.

You are light.

You are love.

And you are destined for greatness.

Go Bravely!

—Dr. Shelly-Ann Gajadhar
L.L.B., L.E.C., MSc., Pg.Dip., PhD

JANUARY

1

Self-mastery rests in loving accountability. The more you hold yourself responsible for your evolution, the more gracefully you will evolve.

JANUARY

2

---

f you want a beautiful garden,
plant a new seed every day.

JANUARY

3

Relationships are a reflection of yourself. We attract what we are, and we can keep out what we aren't.

JANUARY

4

The human race is here to evolve. Honor what past generations did for us and celebrate the opportunity to do what they could not.

JANUARY

5

Be less afraid of being judged and more afraid of being silenced.

JANUARY

6

———

To avoid delays, do not do more than the day can hold. Approach each day with kindness and reverence for its capacity.

JANUARY

7

Be the wild-spirited, gentle, trailblazing soul that you are. The world will adjust.

JANUARY

8

Contrary to popular opinion, leaders are not only born - they wake up every day and choose to lead.

JANUARY

9

Send love to all those you have lost. Although these individuals have departed, do not neglect the energetic connection you still have with them. Though physicality is temporary, energy is eternal.

JANUARY

10

———

Living a life of flow requires a still mind and actions made from grace and compassion.

JANUARY

11

Creative energy will always yield a positive result. Foster a spirit of allowance and give yourself space to trust your creative expression.

JANUARY

12

Seek the embodiment of your highest self as a lifestyle. Live out the blessing you are - and the blessing you seek to be to others.

JANUARY

13

Hold tight to the vision of the person you desire to be, making a daily effort to embody them.

JANUARY

14

———

When you deeply understand what you bring to the table, you realize and find peace in knowing that you do not need to sit at every table.

JANUARY

15

Getting the most out of your life rests in the set of practices you cultivate and repeat daily. As you change and improve your habits, you transform and enhance your life.

JANUARY

16

You are a blessing to everyone you encounter just by showing up and being the best you possible.

JANUARY

17

Forgiveness is the gateway to letting go of all that does not serve your highest good. Want to exercise forgiveness? Start by forgiving yourself.

JANUARY

18

Identify your life mantra. Before going to bed, ask yourself: "Did I live out my life mantra today?"

JANUARY

19

Stop trying to convince others of the role you play in their lives. Honor your assignment and role well. The universe sees it all.

JANUARY

20

B efore you engage in an argument, first take a calming breath and look for the lesson in the disagreement.

JANUARY

21

Want to know if you are in full alignment with your higher vibration? Do an audit on what your body is trying to tell you, letting it unearth the patterns that no longer serve you.

JANUARY

22

To be influential, you must be okay with speaking truth to power. It is better to lose one to the truth than keep a thousand disillusioned.

JANUARY

23

Self-promotion is a celebration of the soul's magnificence. Remember: the world does not know what you offer if you do not announce it.

JANUARY

24

Whenever there is outflow, there is sure to be inflow. Make every expense and purchase with a sense of joy, knowing you are opening yourself to receive equal or greater abundance.

JANUARY

25

With every life milestone, we grow and conquer a piece of fear until all that is left of that mountain is a memory.

JANUARY

26

Confidence increases when competencies are strengthened. As you commit to daily self-improvement, you garner the momentum that leads to personal breakthroughs and success.

JANUARY

27

If you seek to be impactful, practice making an impact. If you seek to be loving, become love. Embody and express the service you seek to give.

JANUARY

28

Passive-aggression is a symptom of a suppressed, silenced, and overlooked voice. You cure yourself when you seek to speak from your heart center.

JANUARY

29

Our lives are characterized by seasons. A season to raise a family, a season to seek promotion, a season to increase wealth. Identify the season you are in and honor it. All this must pass to give birth to something new.

JANUARY

30

To receive a clear guiding signal of guidance from your inner voice, dedicate a day to the purification of your thoughts, your diet, and your environment. Make space for the message to land.

JANUARY

31

It's never too late to start something new. Let not your age or your ego's idea of time stop you from dreaming a new dream and creating a new world for yourself.

FEBRUARY

1

With each new month, I deepen my commitment to purpose and shed my attachment to doubt.

FEBRUARY

2

Productivity rests in how often we feel energized by what we have to do. A simple way to feel energized by your task is to remind yourself of your "why."

FEBRUARY

3

———

We seek change but fear failing, oblivious to the fact that our unhappy circumstances are, themselves, a state of failure. Make the change and take the leap.

FEBRUARY

4

Make a habit of reframing the mind's pessimistic outlook. Both the good and bad of life are here to teach you something.

FEBRUARY

5

———

By celebrating your strengths, accomplishments, and victories, you become a shining example of radical self-love.

FEBRUARY

6

Being an influential leader is having the ability to compassionately meet people where they are and lead them to where they want and deserve to be.

FEBRUARY

7

Your business is your sacred offering to this world. Protect it, celebrate it, show up for it, honor it.

FEBRUARY

8

When you start to do more for yourself and less for everyone else, you feel the weight of everyone else's expectations fall away. Finally, you can feel the lightness of your own spirit. You are free.

FEBRUARY

9

When we do anything halfway, we only cheat ourselves out of the opportunity to go beyond our limits and into higher levels of greatness. Whatever you do, give it your all or don't do it all. The best things require your best effort.

FEBRUARY

10

You are not incompetent; you are just unwilling. Unwilling to follow your heart. Unwilling to answer your calling. Unwilling to subject yourself to criticism. Life is ready to gift you the will to succeed, but you must first be willing to get out of your own way.

FEBRUARY

11

It may be painful. It may cause you tears. It may stir up fear. But remember, life wants to grow you. Life takes care of life.

FEBRUARY

12

Every day is an opportunity to do better, and grace to get it right.

FEBRUARY

13

The act of self-giving is the greatest form of communion with the Divine. What you give to yourself, give first to God.

FEBRUARY

14

———

You are more expansive than even your own imagination. You are the universe, the cosmos, and everything that the Divine is.

FEBRUARY

15

It can get tiring running around
in a costume that doesn't fit.
Remove each piece, layer by layer
-truth lies underneath.

FEBRUARY

16

It's a beautiful thing when purpose and passion align. One purpose can be fulfilled through multiple passions.

FEBRUARY

17

Be like water—flow without reservation, gently creating a wave of openness.
Rest in your essence.

FEBRUARY

18

———

C ourage is knowing that you are not ready, but you will do it anyway because life is ready.

FEBRUARY

19

Kindness is a sweet fragrance welcoming you into love and treating you with compassion.

FEBRUARY

20

Take a deep breath in and feel your lungs being renewed as your ribs open up to receive life. What a beautiful living specimen you are.

FEBRUARY

21

The trauma of your parents is not yours to carry but rather yours to lovingly bury. A new narrative starts with you.

FEBRUARY

22

Be proud of the small wins: waking up on time, putting the trash out, or showing up to work with enthusiasm. You are a walking success!

FEBRUARY

23

Just as light illuminates dark places, so can you brighten up this world. Truth is your identity, and light is your nature.

FEBRUARY

24

Beautiful woman, the stars look down on you in awe of the color of your skin and your natural crown. They keep wondering if you are one of them.

FEBRUARY

25

Your vulnerability
will set you free.

FEBRUARY

26

You can receive pleasure
only in portion to
your inner healing.

FEBRUARY

27

A powerful reminder:
God strengthens
you to do all things.

FEBRUARY

28

It's okay to surrender to the things you can't control. It's not okay to be lackadaisical with the things you can control.

MARCH

1

It's a new month, and I welcome this day with joy, enthusiasm, and bravery. I choose to be right here, right now—exactly where I am.

MARCH

2

Like a seed, all thoughts germinate in fertile soil. Keep the soil of your mind nourished with positive and progress-oriented thoughts.

MARCH

3

Lean not on your own understanding. There is guidance stronger than the limitations of the mind. Feel. Let your heart process this one.

MARCH

4

You don't choose your dreams. Your dreams choose you.

MARCH

5

I n difficult situations, pray.
Prayer has a powerful way of
shifting difficulty to acceptance
and resistance to surrender.

MARCH

6

You are light. You are love. You are destined for greatness. Yes, you!

MARCH

7

lead with love. I speak with love.
I anoint myself with love. Love is
the sweet fragrance I exude.

MARCH

8

Failing once does not mean you're incompetent. It only means there are ninety-nine more options to try. Don't give up!

MARCH

9

You are here to change your own narrative. I pray infinite blessings on the beautiful energy shifts you've made mentally and physically.

MARCH

10

Quit forcing the relationships and connections that your spirit finds deeply draining. Your body vessel, mind, and sacred soul all deserve peace.

MARCH

11

Go where you are celebrated. Stay where it's consistent. Grow in loving reciprocation.

MARCH

12

A gentle reminder: be gentle with yourself. You are doing the best you can with the life you have.

MARCH

13

———

Those beautiful hips and luscious lips echo an eternal truth: that everything about you is simply divine.

MARCH

14

Attempt to see God in everything, not because your faith is perfect, but because your life is a glowing testimony to the constant presence of a Higher Power.

MARCH

15

—————

Failure is a part of your human design and evolution. To be afraid to fail is to be afraid to evolve.

MARCH

16

L ife's got you. You've made it this far. There is still life energy dancing inside of you. Now, rest in the warm knowledge that God has always cared for you.

MARCH

17

Confuse not your heart with the trials of life. Life takes care of life, and life shall surely take care of you.

MARCH

18

Your desire to be loved is your yearning to experience your own love. Love is you.

MARCH

19

Be convinced of your ability to self-preserve. You came into this world kicking and screaming. Tap into the fighter in you.

MARCH

20

If no one told you, you are like a shining temple. Petals should be laid at your feet.

MARCH

21

Take your success slowly. You've got to be willing to crawl before you walk. You've got to be willing to walk before you run.

MARCH

22

t's a beautiful thing when a passion becomes a profession. Believe in the magic of possibility.

MARCH

23

Every day is a good day to spread love. Feel love pouring into you. See it overflowing. Now, visualize yourself joyfully sharing it.

MARCH

24

Love is boundless. It does not give and take. It is not a transaction.

MARCH

25

Instead of waiting for the words you yearn to hear to flow from the lips of another, listen to the unspoken word. Like a waterfall, it flows the loudest.

MARCH

26

Our relationships reflect where we are in this moment of life. Make yourself proud.

MARCH

27

Life becomes difficult when we seek to control all things. Surrender to that which is higher than you. You will find the burdens you carry become lighter.

MARCH

28

To know thyself is to love thyself. To love thyself is to know thyself. No one knows how to love you like you do.

MARCH

29

Be meticulous with your mind garden. Prune unruly flowers and unearth pestering weeds. Too much of anything leads to imbalance.

MARCH

30

Celebrate your small wins. Sometimes the applause you need to hear the most comes from your own hands.

APRIL

1

Your hurt can bury you
or resurrect you.
With the spoken word,
compel your mind, body, and
soul to be resurrected.

APRIL

2

What you believe you are, you are. What you say you are, you are.

APRIL

3

When we grow, we shed. When we shed, we renew. Honor the pruning of the past and the blooming of the present.

APRIL

4

Become so engrossed in your happiness that another's happiness is confirmation of what is headed to you.

APRIL

5

welcome in love. I see with the
eyes of love. Everything I do,
I do it with love. Now, repeat.

APRIL

6

Money follows; it never leads. Are you doing things that command money to follow you? Whatever you do, make sure joy is included. Money, success, and opulence all follow joy.

APRIL

7

There is a limit to our own self-healing. Sometimes your healing calls for openness, receptivity, and another soul to open the parts of your heart you are incapable of opening.

APRIL

8

Watch out for the subtlety of discrimination. It can come across as a light-hearted joke that leaves your heart heavy.

APRIL

9

Don't take yourself so seriously. Play! The world goes on with or without you.

APRIL

10

Enthusiasm is a powerful ingredient for manifestation. Greet the day with enthusiasm. Be enthusiastic about the big and small occurrences in your life. Your life IS exciting!

APRIL

11

Visualize your inner child. Give her a hug. You are her, and she is you.

APRIL

12

Move to the beat of your soul today. Whatever it sounds like, find the rhythm and give a little sway.

APRIL

13

Losing a loved one is painful. Chaining them to this realm in grief is suffering. Lovingly release. They deserve to dance in the next realm.

APRIL

14

The world will chastise you for celebrating yourself. Your soul will praise you for doing it anyway.

APRIL

15

A hundred "no's" narrow the balance of probabilities for a "yes." Keep applying pressure.

APRIL

16

You're not here just to work. You're also here to play, enjoy, and live.

APRIL

17

Grief is the one emotion that deeply reminds us of our temporary nature.

APRIL

18

Not everyone will speak
your love language.
Ask for what you seek.

APRIL

19

Just because we leave people behind does not mean we forget about them. Give gratitude for the role they played in your growth process.

APRIL

20

When you stop tiptoeing around your potential, you'll also stop tiptoeing around the naysayers.

APRIL

21

Friendship calls for one true skill: the art of listening without judgment.

APRIL

22

You have all the tools you need to succeed. Life has cared for you in your mediocrity. Why wouldn't life also take care of you in your abundance?

APRIL

23

Courage isn't always loud.
It can also be silent,
observant, and calculated.

APRIL

24

There is bliss in not responding to every distracting thought or provoking word. Your attention should not be so cheap.

APRIL

25

We have gotten into the habit of seeking happiness. Choose fulfillment instead.

APRIL

26

Self-love is a ritual. It is a slow and gentle dance with your flaws.

APRIL

27

It is not that you lack discipline; you only lack motivation. Be motivated to overcome the test and battles of your lowest self. Your highest expression of life will emerge when you are disciplined.

APRIL

28

Growth occurs where you direct energy. You want more love; give more energy to receiving love. You desire more money; give more energy to income-generating things. Whatever you desire needs your attention.

APRIL

29

I n this world filled with criticism, choose to be the defender of your dreams. Quit leaving them helpless and bullied.

APRIL

30

Whenever you feel worried, reflect on how far you've come. Your life is a beautiful track record of overcoming.

MAY

1

Practice gratitude every day. You have risen to see another sunrise. Give thanks!

MAY

2

Hard decisions become easy when we earnestly follow the genuine desires of our hearts.

MAY

3

———

You're not always going to get it right; that's human error. Be thankful for your humanness.

MAY

4

Transfiguration is changing inwardly to accommodate life's changes. May we all welcome the process.

MAY

5

Stop trying to manage time. Time will do as it must. Instead, intentionally manage your tasks. Be a master at how you move throughout time and space with dedication, focus, ease and grace.

MAY

6

We all have a story inside of us. Share at least one line today. Someone needs to hear it.

MAY

7

Fear arrives in our attempts to control something beyond our control. What are you attempting to control? Release it, and let fear go on its way.

MAY

8

—————

All that we are required to do is our best. Give your best. That's all that is expected.

MAY

9

———

Believe in yourself so deeply that it inspires others to believe in themselves, too.

MAY

10

The things we believe we lack are not necessary in this moment. Right now, we lack nothing. The moment is full—meet it in your fullness.

MAY

11

Your parents did the best they could with the best they had. Honor that.

MAY

12

We tend to use today's wisdom to judge yesterday. How unreasonable! Be kind to yourself.

MAY

13

Observe how children play unreservedly. Tap into their nature. Let not adulthood make you rigid.

MAY

14

Appreciate that someone's negativity is a projection of what they lack. Witness—but do not absorb and become—what you see.

MAY

15

———

If you can visualize it, then you can manifest it. Put some action behind those prayers.

MAY

16

Not everyone will celebrate your joy. This is part of their story, not yours.

MAY

17

Display activism in all aspects of your life: work, family, love, and play. Demonstrate your passion and zeal.

MAY

18

We get out of life that which we courageously ask for.

MAY

19

When anxiety wells up, ask yourself: what am I trying to control that is beyond my control? Remember that the uncontrollable future, must not have the power to control you in the here and now.

MAY

20

It is not enough to walk through a garden of roses. Stretch your fingers out and make a connection with life. Feel life at your fingertips.

MAY

21

Your love language is beautiful, and someone out there is fluent in it. Keep believing!

MAY

22

Friends are like puzzle pieces—
no two are the same. And each
friend is an essential piece to
the intricate puzzle that is you.

MAY

23

Throughout your day, keep God in your thoughts. This is a form of simple meditation without the yoga mat.

MAY

24

When we greet our days with a smile, we give the day a wave of gratitude. Life smiles on you every day. Why not smile back?

MAY

25

You have choices. You have options. You are boundless potential.

MAY

26

Rage can disconnect us from love. Unforgiveness can disconnect us from empathy.

MAY

27

You are a rare being. A unique contradiction. You do not need to be accepted. You simply need to be experienced. Your presence is a lesson for the world.

MAY

28

Rebellion creates acrimony.
Revolution creates alchemy.

MAY

29

It's not only about how we move through our light; it's also about how we move through our darkness. Find your vibration of kindness.

MAY

30

The right people know your ailments before your diagnosis.

MAY

31

Let your life existence be an uninhibited dance in bliss, a soul-nurturing celebration honoring your growth.

JUNE

1

We are afraid to be judged by others, so we dim our lights, not realizing that we have first judged ourselves.

JUNE

2

Take a moment and
give yourself a big hug!
Sometimes your body needs
to be reminded of your own touch.

JUNE

3

Create a spiritual practice, if you haven't already. Your healing requires your devotion.

JUNE

4

Invigorate the soul by
doing something out of the
ordinary. Remind the soul
what it means to live.

JUNE

5

Life has chosen you for its experience and expression. Use your gifts to tell the tale.

JUNE

6

Trust your gut more.
It's giving you a bit of
wisdom in advance.

JUNE

7

Never forget to pray for your business and goals. They, too, need communion with God.

JUNE

8

———

Be wary of friendly competition. That which starts amicably has the propensity to become hostile.

JUNE

9

The wisdom you now possess is healing medicine for your past traumas. It should not be misused as an instrument for self-judgment.

JUNE

10

In conflict, listen with the desire to understand rather than respond.

JUNE

11

We create worlds with our words. Create for yourself a world of love, compassion, and grace.

JUNE

12

Recognize your darkness; the parts of you hidden away from judgment. After all, darkness can only exist where there is also light.

JUNE

13

Avoid responding according to the world's expectations for your existence. Instead, choose to be proactive and aligned with your soul's mission.

JUNE

14

When you believe you are worthy, every atom responds and assimilates to your worthy desires.

JUNE

15

Not every change needs an explanation. Sometimes, it simply requires observation.

JUNE

16

Find your inner silence. That place of peace, warmth, and loving compassion. In times of difficulty, go there.

JUNE

17

Have the courage to make the difficult choices of life. These decisions help us live in the space of intention.

JUNE

18

Listen well while resisting agreement with the negative projections of others. Simply respond with: "That's interesting." Be allured by—not aligned with—how people think.

JUNE

19

"I am a work in progress. The work is never complete until my time on Earth is over."

JUNE

20

———

The act of speaking allows you to release and express. When you use the sacred word, ask yourself: "Am I speaking from a place of love? Are my words sacred?" Remember: you create worlds with your words.

JUNE

21

Your happiness overflows when you break past the limits of your own expectations.

JUNE

22

Give your love space and time to grow. An overzealous hand can lead to an overwhelmed interaction.

JUNE

23

Recognize when a once safe spaces become unsafe. This is a call for you to ascend.

JUNE

24

The magic in life is seated in the enthusiasm you bring to each day.

JUNE

25

Don't take yesterday or tomorrow to bed with you.

JUNE

26

———

Dance or sing a song at least once every day.

JUNE

27

The spiritually minded know which aspects of their life need soothing, and they gracefully commit to its treatment.

JUNE

28

Having difficulty making career, education, or business decisions? Simply ask yourself: what is the return on my investment for my time, energy, or resources?

JUNE

29

Resist sulking in disappointment when friends and family do not support your endeavors. You are pursuing your goals for a much bigger cause that overshadows such disappointment.

JUNE

30

———

Never disempower yourself with the words, "I can't." Instead, replace these words with: "I am struggling with;" "I am encountering difficulty with;" or "I am having a challenging time with." Your words provide the power to overcome!

JULY

1

Your purpose is not defined by a worldly role, position, or title. It is a deep desire with a simple explanation. Most times, service to others is a key ingredient.

JULY

2

Your world changes for the better when you break the habit of absorbing the frequency of others and start emitting your own.

JULY

3

Joyfully greet the day in gratitude. Just as you can charge your crystals with the rays of the sun, you can also charge your life with the light of loving words.

JULY

4

———————

Our desires are within reach. To be a magnet for what you seek, you must first embody that which you desire.

JULY

5

"Market saturation" just means the world demands that many hands. All living things carry a divine role. Know yours.

JULY

6

Inspirational leadership first starts
with good self-leadership.

JULY

7

Remove the comparison. Recognize that we are all reflecting each other in magical ways!

JULY

8

How you view your challenges will determine how much discomfort you experience. See life's challenges as opportunities for victory rather than a sure path to defeat.

JULY

9

Your mind is filled with an infinite number of thoughts each day, and your dreams struggle to find a safe space to stay. Give your dreams protection and rest. Write them out.

JULY

10

Pay attention to the signs all around you. Life isn't happening coincidentally. Life is happening for you, intentionally.

JULY

11

Give healing freely. A warm smile, an embracing hug, a kind word. You are walking soul medicine.

JULY

12

To appreciate the elements of earth, air, water, and fire is to deeply appreciate your human nature.

JULY

13

Y ou will receive many "no's;"
refuse to accept them
as the final answer.

JULY

14

"Money exists in abundance. I am a vessel for wealth, prosperity, and luxury."

JULY

15

Beauty is a feeling. It isn't found in your timelines or in the latest trends, but in your loving acceptance of self.

JULY

16

———

Your feet reflect your self-care state. Lovingly look at your feet. What are they saying?

JULY

17

D ance like no one is watching!
Move your body, gyrate
your hips, raise the vibration
of your body vessel. Make every
movement today sacred.

JULY

18

We think we should not experience problems, but our problems prepare us for what life wants to show us.

JULY

19

S eek out that person who sparks inspiration or joy inside of you. Mentorship can be found both near and far.

JULY

20

Most of us are living out someone else's dream. Don't let life pass you by without having lived your own.

JULY

21

Never bury your past. Instead, appreciate its role and lovingly set it free.

JULY

22

I am so proud of you. You are healing, forgiving, and growing. That's beautiful!

JULY

23

Believe that you have the power to change your habits. You did it as a child. You can also do it in adulthood.

JULY

24

When you lack inspiration, remember its source flows through you. What is the story in your heart you'd like to tell?

JULY

25

Many of the things we lack are only absent because we do not ask with intention.

JULY

26

Lovingly affirm someone today. The more you pour out love, the more you prepare yourself to receive love.

JULY

27

Changing the world starts with changing the way we operate within it. When people experience you, be a loving reminder of the peace and power within them.

JULY

28

The difference between fear and intuition is separation. Fear separates you; intuition connects you.

JULY

29

Healing is a lifelong journey.
No need to rush it.

JULY

30

Your business has an identity of its own; a vision larger than your own comprehension and a purpose greater than your fears.

JULY

31

Take a moment today to hug yourself. Warmly embrace your body. What a resilient being you are!

AUGUST

1

Life is in all things. Life seeks to bring forth life, and your life will do the same.

AUGUST

2

Maintain your inner peace by accepting that you are not here to change minds; you are here to give perspective. Your existence is the lesson.

AUGUST

3

Dare to be your highest self. The world needs this version of you.

AUGUST

4

Practice hope. As hope becomes a habit, our desires become easier to manifest.

AUGUST

5

The mind is a womb. What you think, you birth.

AUGUST

6

We all serve each other in this world. The world itself functions on the foundation of service. Whatever you do, do it as a service, and let service lead you to success.

AUGUST

7

In the moments when creativity feels blocked, look around. Everything that exists around you is creativity in motion.

AUGUST

8

Not every divine message gifted to you is intended for public consumption. Sometimes, it's for your heart and mind only.

AUGUST

9

When you give yourself permission to be you, all the lights in your world suddenly turn on.

AUGUST

10

When you pray, pray big. For nothing is too small for God.

AUGUST

11

Decide you are worthy of the same time you spend serving others. Self-care takes time.

AUGUST

12

Every day is an opportunity to release the false stories you've told about yourself.

AUGUST

13

We cause ourselves much pain and suffering when we try to control everything. Allow the Divine space to intercede.

AUGUST

14

Your life does not change with one decision. Your life changes when you commit to the decision.

AUGUST

15

———

Attempting to stop the chatter in your mind can be an endless pursuit. Instead, simply monitor the dialogue you have with your thoughts.

AUGUST

16

Don't forget to feel today. Feel your way through this season. Feel your way through these tests. Feel your way toward the things that allow you to feel good about where you are.

AUGUST

17

The road to success can be arduous. Never forget why you chose this journey. Your "why" is your roadmap.

AUGUST

18

You are walking wealth.

AUGUST

19

———

There are twenty-four hours in a day—1,440 minutes. Surely, your self-care is worthy of some time.

AUGUST

20

Clothe yourself in fabrics that raise your vibration. Command this realm in style. You deserve nothing less!

AUGUST

21

Endeavor to see the positive possibility in all things. All things are working for your good.

AUGUST

22

Free yourself of the trials of the day. Just as the sun sets for rest, so, too, should you.

AUGUST

23

Y ou have the power to handle difficult situations with grace. Do not allow your intolerance or impatience to tell you otherwise.

AUGUST

24

Hurt is part of the human process. So, too, is healing. Both require time.

AUGUST

25

If you seek to be more spiritually strong, fill your gaps of time with growth.

AUGUST

26

A person's reaction to your behavior is theirs. Your reaction to their behavior is yours. It's not what people do that needs analyzing; it's how you watch them.

AUGUST

27

The people who need the most love from us usually express it in the most unkind ways. Love them fiercely!

AUGUST

28

"My life is a reflection of harmony and balance. I am in harmony with all things.

AUGUST

29

Entrepreneurs, your friendship is the paycheck to your friends. Your business is their bonus.

AUGUST

30

t's okay to change your mind, plans, and direction. Life is in constant motion, and so are you.

AUGUST

31

Shine so brightly that your rays of light provide sunshine to your loved ones. Be the beacon.

SEPTEMBER

1

Whatever you love doing, love it deeply. It can transform you, if you let it.

SEPTEMBER

2

You serve no one by placing yourself in a box. The world needs your creative expression. Share your gifts and let the divine creative energy flow through you freely.

SEPTEMBER

3

Be your own guinea pig. Test your ideas, troubleshoot your projects. Be the student and the teacher.

SEPTEMBER

4

Don't be so quick to weed people out of your life. Sometimes, the relationship is a rose in need of pruning.

SEPTEMBER

5

Get out of the habit of thinking you need to fill all your roles at once. Sometimes, life is calling you to focus on one role in this moment. Trust the timing of your life.

SEPTEMBER

6

Embrace your tears. They are a testimony that your stone-cold hurt is liquifying and releasing.

SEPTEMBER

7

Ritualize your relationships. Let your service to them reflect your service to the Divine.

SEPTEMBER

8

Focus on the steps you're taking toward greatness. The destination requires preparation.

SEPTEMBER

9

S aying no does not equate to losing the relationship. Instead, saying no creates loving boundaries and healthier relationships.

SEPTEMBER

10

D on't give away all your
yeses to the world.
Save a yes for you!

SEPTEMBER

11

Difficult situations don't need your irritated response. Most times, they need your calm compassion.

SEPTEMBER

12

Your dreams just need you to start. Remember: progress, not perfection.

SEPTEMBER

13

The higher your vibration, the more clearly you see the world's challenges. We can't ask for sunshine without the heat.

SEPTEMBER

14

When God illuminates your purpose, you no longer mince matters with your existence.

SEPTEMBER

15

Show up for yourself before anyone else does. Be the coach, the cheerleader, and the player!

SEPTEMBER

16

Wherever attention goes, energy flows. Guide your attention to peace and prosperity. Claim it!

SEPTEMBER

17

Don't be so worried about being accepted. You are not a commodity; you are an experience.

SEPTEMBER

18

surrender to the
magic stored in today.

SEPTEMBER

19

A wise woman commenced her healing journey. A wiser woman lived her healing journey.

SEPTEMBER

20

As money comes to you, pay yourself first. After all, your existence attracted the money in the first place.

SEPTEMBER

21

You can easily ritualize your days by seeing every action and movement as a form of meditation.

SEPTEMBER

22

Do not be so quick to judge. All that we witness, we are meant to witness. It is all part of our healing and the story we tell.

SEPTEMBER

23

They may laugh today, but later they may ask for the recipe. Keep on keeping on!

SEPTEMBER

24

Release the anger—it keeps us in the past. Gratitude keeps us in the present moment.

SEPTEMBER

25

There is healing energy flowing through your hands. Wherever you need tender care, gently place your hands there.

SEPTEMBER

26

D ifficult moments can be overcome by the breath. Deeply inhale your peace and exhale your tension.

SEPTEMBER

27

You do not need to do everything now. Whatever life needs in this very moment, be present with that.

SEPTEMBER

28

We all need a role model—a person who can remind us of our infinite possibility.

SEPTEMBER

29

Service to others does not require losing your dignity or handing over ownership of self.

SEPTEMBER

30

In all actions, ask yourself:
"What space am I taking
this action from?"

OCTOBER

1

Move through life's challenges with bountiful grace and a heart that holds no grudges.

OCTOBER

2

There is no lack of money.
Rather, there is a lack of
demand and command for it.

OCTOBER

3

Do not allow disagreements to create animosity. Instead, let them be a gentle reminder of how uniquely different we all are.

OCTOBER

4

The things that trigger you are indicators of what needs healing. When triggered, ask yourself: "What pain is this connected to?"

OCTOBER

5

We limit our boundlessness when we rigidly attach ourselves to the roles we play. You are more than the role.

OCTOBER

6

It's not that you don't have enough time; you are unreasonable with the time you have. Invest more time in the things that light you up and make you forget about time altogether. From here, time will be a servant to you.

OCTOBER

7

Life is rhythmic. Your routines, habits, and lifestyle produce a melody that will either encourage success or foster stagnation.

OCTOBER

8

Consideration is the
forefather of compassion.

OCTOBER

9

It's okay to take your talent seriously. Just be sure you aren't taking yourself too seriously.

OCTOBER

10

———

Be gentle with yourself.
Only then can you be
gentle with others.

OCTOBER

11

Ideas are many, but the execution of them is rare. Those who take action will be remembered.

OCTOBER

12

You are the beginning and the end. There is no need to rush your unfolding.

OCTOBER

13

Let your words be sweet like honey. Let your deeds be kind and lovely.

OCTOBER

14

Have a goal you'd like to achieve? Commit to doing at least one thing every day that will help you achieve it. Remember that a journey of thousand miles starts with one step.

OCTOBER

15

Do not be afraid to bring your monetary requests to God in prayer. The Divine is the Source of all things, including your financial abundance.

OCTOBER

16

Upgrade the vocabulary used to describe your life. Replace the word "boasting" with "celebrating."

OCTOBER

17

Your boundaries need not always be a sword that decapitates those who cross them. They can also be a loving "no" signaling that you will be treated with reverence.

OCTOBER

18

If you are having a hard time waking up early, cultivate an inviting morning flow that honors, rather than jolts, your body. Create an experience that the body can look forward to when it awakens.

OCTOBER

19

I am love. I see love. I exude love. I embody love. I am love.

OCTOBER

20

The biggest thing standing between you and your dreams is the decision to not take positive action in your life. We take action every day, but not every action is positive.

OCTOBER

21

When you allow your heart to feel, you become more connected to the present moment; it is a portal into the eternal now.

OCTOBER

22

Anger keeps us rooted in the past. Worry keeps us in the future. Gratitude keeps us anchored in the now.

OCTOBER

23

Do not allow the limited definitions of a work title to define you. If you are an assistant but have the energy of a manager, then embody that. Regardless of title, be the highest you!

OCTOBER

24

Pretending we're fine creates a dangerous habit of growing into our traumas instead of our healing.

OCTOBER

25

Every morning, before your mind attempts to dictate the day's events, guide your body through a sweet awakening. The mind demands, but the body endures.

OCTOBER

26

Let comparison inspire you to lovingly appreciate what you are and what you are not.

OCTOBER

27

Take a trip to an unknown place. Attempt something new. Take a risk. Don't allow the world to be the only challenging force in your life. Challenge yourself on your terms.

OCTOBER

28

I f you desire more wealth, practice
increasing your energetic
capacity to hold and sustain
such wealth. Attune yourself to
holding that voltage.

OCTOBER

29

Forgive yourself for the times you did not get it right. Mistakes are a part of this human experience.

OCTOBER

30

The lies we tell others are also the lies we tell ourselves. May we have the courage to get free. Reminder: Only the truth will set you free! Speak your truth and live it too.

OCTOBER

31

Y ou serve people not only with your presence but also with your absence. If your life asks for stillness, listen, and know that showing up for you is also showing up for others.

NOVEMBER

1

Find time to dance this week. Life is rhythmic, and its melodies are always inviting you to the dance floor.

NOVEMBER

2

Everything necessary to sustain you in this world is within reach. All you have to do is release the false ego and make your request.

NOVEMBER

3

Sometimes our dreams take forever to get off the ground because we never fully commit to their takeoff.

NOVEMBER

4

I f we see time as eternal, then we must appreciate that it cannot be controlled. How we experience time is up to us. Set an intention for time and enjoy each passing tick.

NOVEMBER

5

To feel the fullness of life is to see yourself in everything. You are everything, and everything is you.

NOVEMBER

6

Creative energy is not to be wasted nor exploited. Act on your creative impulse and rest when tiredness comes.

NOVEMBER

7

Take a moment to close your eyes and feel your heartbeat. Feel the wind gently brush your face. Feel the sun's rays warm your body. To feel your presence, simply be present.

NOVEMBER

8

In this life, death is certain. We fully experience life by making positive decisions in uncertainty—decisions that help us grow.

NOVEMBER

9

Your perceived inadequacy is temporary. Remember, everything you seem to lack is reachable.

NOVEMBER

10

You're not always going to get it right. Part of the experience is getting it wrong, troubleshooting ways to get it right, and challenging yourself beyond your comfort zones.

NOVEMBER

11

———————

When conflicts arise—as they always do—resolve them by remembering the shared goal. Oftentimes, it's the conflicting approach that is the problem, not the individual.

NOVEMBER

12

When implementing loving boundaries, remember: they aren't just for you. They are also helping others to become more compassionate, emotionally intelligent, and receptive to harmonious co-existence.

NOVEMBER

13

Your passion feels burdensome when you start characterizing it by someone else's standards. Allow your passion to do what it does best. It does not need you as a chaperone.

NOVEMBER

14

As you wake up every morning, gently repeat the word "victory" in your mind. Let the vibration of the word ignite your day.

NOVEMBER

15

Your business requires your devotion. You do not plant the seed and eat the fruit on the same day.

NOVEMBER

16

What we do for others, we also do for ourselves. Through service to others, we perform a service to ourselves.

NOVEMBER

17

"I am enough." Three simple words, when said with meaning, energize your entire being.

NOVEMBER

18

When a loved one crosses your mind, pick up the phone and give them a call or send them a text. Don't miss the opportunity to let those you care about know they are appreciated.

NOVEMBER

19

Confidence does not want to be accepted; it simply wants to be expressed.

NOVEMBER

20

You don't need to respond to every rude remark. Observation is the foundation of building character.

NOVEMBER

21

Find a space where it's safe enough for you to share your big dreams. Your dreams require community.

NOVEMBER

22

Be proud of the spaces you've left behind in order to become a person worthy of the spaces you desire to fill. Thank you for being courageous.

NOVEMBER

23

You can be a sage and still be unwelcome. There is wisdom in knowing what we can't be for everyone.

NOVEMBER

24

Whenever you feel confused, place your hands on your heart center. Ask your heart to show you the way. It is a reliable compass.

NOVEMBER

25

Y ou don't have to wait on someone to buy you flowers. Go out and buy your own. There is something deeply intimate about loving on you.

NOVEMBER

26

Confidence is like a muscle; it can only be built by intentional exertion and practice.

NOVEMBER

27

It's okay if there aren't many people doing what you do. It's an opportunity for you to pave the way.

NOVEMBER

28

Beware of people who chastise you rather than celebrate you. They can make your dreams seem elusive.

NOVEMBER

29

Acknowledge your ability
to get up after every
fall. You survived.

NOVEMBER

30

Others respect you when you respect yourself. Ask yourself: "What does self-respect look like to me?" Whatever your answer is, do that.

DECEMBER

1

Visualize opportunities all around you. Remember, once you have breath, you have opportunity.

DECEMBER

2

You can feel when life is ready to turn the page to a new chapter. Resistance only leads to suffering. Pray for a sweet surrender.

DECEMBER

3

Do not be afraid to testify what God has done in your life. You open yourself up to more blessings when you do so.

DECEMBER

4

———

Tough environments can be temporary. Affirm daily that this isn't your permanent reality.

DECEMBER

5

Don't be so afraid to fail that you are blinded by the reality of failing situations. Stay present.

DECEMBER

6

Before you open your eyes every morning, take a moment to smile at the day. Let it be a smile of appreciation. Life chose you.

DECEMBER

7

Always keep a list of your achievements—the things you are most proud of. This can be a confidence booster in times of self-doubt.

DECEMBER

8

You don't have to find purpose. Purpose is already inside of you. Remove expectations and allow purpose to pour out of you.

DECEMBER

9

Being productive in life requires creating a system of organization for your tasks and resisting distractions that divert your focus. Both are challenging.

DECEMBER

10

It's not always going to be easy. Some days you will feel like giving up. On those days, remind yourself that the challenge is here to grow you. Grow.

DECEMBER

11

———————

Avoid listening to people who say you can't do something. Their reality, capability, and vision are not yours.

DECEMBER

12

Progress is a big component of this earthly experience. Every day is an opportunity to progress in whatever little ways we can.

DECEMBER

13

If you keep complaining about something that's missing, consider: maybe you are the person to fill that missing space.

DECEMBER

14

You can feel when someone or someplace is not for you. Trust this feeling and lovingly exit with grace—and gratitude for the revelation.

DECEMBER

15

———

We may not all share the same standards, beliefs, or values. Differences should not be a scapegoat for disrespect.

DECEMBER

16

How you learn from your mistakes and apply those lessons to your daily life says a lot about your character; it's what wisdom is made of.

DECEMBER

17

Take care of your health and wellbeing. You need endurance to achieve the dream inside you.

DECEMBER

18

We can never place a price tag on our worth, but we can place a value on our effort.

DECEMBER

19

If habits are not sticking with you, you aren't the problem—the unreasonableness is.

DECEMBER

20

If you can see the vision, then it is already written. Before you take the next step, know that you already succeeded.

DECEMBER

21

We often think our actions are for other people. Know that your actions are also for you. You are playing your role. Well done!

DECEMBER

22

Start walking like you're blessed, talking like you're blessed, and believing that you are blessed. Miracles are activated by this simple exercise.

DECEMBER

23

You may stir up insecurity in other people as you share your gifts. Someone else's "I can't" is your "I can."

DECEMBER

24

As you experience success, celebrate the tough times and experiences that molded you. Never forget where you came from and what made you, you.

DECEMBER

25

"Today, I want for nothing.
Today, I exercise gratitude."

DECEMBER

26

Appreciate those who support and love you. Let them know you appreciate them in return.

DECEMBER

27

Resentment is not yours to carry. Open your heart and receive love. Open your heart and give forgiveness.

DECEMBER

28

A positive attitude can automatically bring light to a dark situation. Hold on to the light that is hope.

DECEMBER

29

Every high-stakes space you enter, you've earned in some way. Your progress is not a coincidence.

DECEMBER

30

When we find someone we're making progress for, we become more invigorated to make progress. Find your person.

DECEMBER

31

Your life is a testimony to the confident overcoming of every difficult hurdle thrown at you. Confidence is always available to you.

AFFIRMATIONS FOR CAREER

I lead a purposeful career.

My career is owned by
me and no one else.

I possess the agency
to create boundless
opportunities for my path.

I affirm that every workspace I
enter will be divinely aligned.

I affirm that I experience
harmonious relationships with
every work colleague I meet.

I affirm that I am acknowledged
and appreciated for my talents.

I affirm that every obstacle
encountered will be handled with
grace and diplomacy.

I lead a purposeful career.

My career is owned by
me and no one else.

All things are working
for my future self.

And so, it is.

AFFIRMATIONS FOR RELATIONSHIPS

I am a beautiful example of love.

Love is my language.

Love is my lifestyle.

Love is my ritual.

I affirm that every word, deed, and thought is infused with love.

I affirm that I give love, and by giving love, I attract love.

I affirm that every relationship I share is housed by love.

I affirm that every problem is solved with love.

I affirm that I communicate
from a space of love.

I affirm that I see
love in everything.

I affirm that I feel love
in every heartbeat.

I am a beautiful example of love,

Living proof that love heals,

A reminder that love
lives inside of me.

I am loved

And so, it is.

AFFIRMATIONS FOR SCHOOL

I am committed to
fulfilling my dreams.

I am committed to a
purposeful future.

With new knowledge comes
new possibilities.

I affirm that I am joyfully
expanding my mind daily.

I affirm that
focus never leaves me.

I affirm that
discipline abides within me.

I affirm that on the
days of weakness, my
strength is renewed.

I affirm that everything
I learn, I retain.

I affirm that I am prepared for
every exam that comes my way.

I affirm that my academic
success is written.

I am committed to
fulfilling my dreams.

I am committed to a
purposeful future.

I am successful in every test.

And so, it is.

AFFIRMATIONS FOR BUSINESS

My business is divinely anointed.

I am a successful entrepreneur.

My clients/customers are happy.

I affirm that my
business is sacred.

I affirm that my
business is purposeful.

I affirm that my business can
provide for me and my family.

I affirm that my
business impacts lives.

I affirm that my business attracts
a team that reflects its values.

I affirm that my business
will grow each year.

I affirm that my business is
creating a positive legacy.

My business is divinely anointed.

I am a successful entrepreneur.

All the needs of my
business shall be met.

And so, it is.

AFFIRMATIONS FOR HEALTH

My body is a sacred vessel.

My body is a powerful portal.

My health is divinely charged.

I affirm that every cell is optimally working.

I affirm that every muscle in my body is restored.

I affirm that every organ in my body is rejuvenated.

I affirm that my skin, my bones, and my tissues are replenished.

I affirm that my
limbs are invigorated.

I affirm that my body is
healed and healing.

I affirm that my body stores
life and is capable.

My body is a sacred vessel.

My body is a powerful portal.

My body is
transformed and healed.

And so, it is.

AFFIRMATIONS
FOR MONEY

Abundance is my birthright.

Financial wealth is my destiny.

I attract prosperity,
opulence, and wealth.

I affirm that money is not an
enemy but an ally.

I affirm that because
wealth lives inside
of me, I attract wealth.

I affirm that income-generating
opportunities are ever-flowing.

I affirm that there is no
financial lack, only surplus.

I affirm that I am a
worthy vessel to make,
receive, and spend money.

I affirm that money works
for me and supports my
dreams and desires.

I affirm that every need of
mine and my loved ones
are financially met.

Abundance is my birthright.

Financial wealth is my destiny.

I am a magnet for prosperity.

And so, it is.

AFFIRMATIONS FOR SPIRITUALITY

I am divinely
created and protected.

My Supreme Being is always
near in times of need.

I am a sacred vessel.

I affirm that the Divine guides my
every thought and action.

I affirm that the principles
of love and compassion
guide my existence.

I affirm that help is
always a prayer away.

I affirm that the Divine is with
me everywhere I go.

I affirm that I can easily
converse with the Divine
as a form of prayer.

I affirm that the Divine lives
within me and in all things.

I affirm that my heart is open and
respectful to all paths.

I affirm that my relationship with
the Divine is unique and personal.

I am divinely
created and protected.

My Supreme Being is always
near in times of need
and watches over me.

And so, it is.

ABOUT
THE AUTHOR

Dr. Shelly-Ann Gajadhar is an Educator, Attorney, and Coach for High-Achievers. Born in Trinidad and Tobago, she has always been an island girl with big dreams. Migrating to the UK at the pinnacle of her career transition from law to academia, she relied heavily on her bravery, resilience, and knowledge to see her dreams through in unfamiliar terrain. She is now the CEO of a global coaching consultancy, Alphastute, and serves as a High-Performance Coach to disruptors, innovators, high-achievers, and thought-leaders.

CPSIA information can be obtained
at www.ICGtesting.com
Printed in the USA
BVHW010104030123
655447BV00023B/287

9 798218 102159